What Is the Story of Captain Kirk?

What Is the Story of Captain Kirk?

by M. D. Payne

illustrated by Robert Squier

Penguin Workshop

To the brightest star in the galaxy,
Stella Dale—MDP

For Chuck, a generally peaceful, sentient
humanoid life form and friend—RS

PENGUIN WORKSHOP
An imprint of Penguin Random House LLC, New York

First published in the United States of America by Penguin Workshop,
an imprint of Penguin Random House LLC, New York, 2021

Visit us online at penguinrandomhouse.com.

Library of Congress Cataloging-in-Publication Data is available.

Printed in the United States of America

ISBN 9781524791148 (paperback)   10 9 8 7 6 5 4 3 2 1 WOR
ISBN 9781524791155 (library binding)   10 9 8 7 6 5 4 3 2 1 WOR

Contents

What Is the Story of Captain Kirk?

On the evening of September 8, 1966, people all around the United States tuned in to the NBC network. They were about to experience a historic moment in TV history: the very first episode of the new science fiction series, *Star Trek*. It was called "The Man Trap."

Viewers saw a spaceship orbiting a red planet.

Then they heard a commanding voice say: "Captain's log, Stardate 1513.1. Our position: orbiting Planet M-113 . . ."

The voice they heard belonged to Captain James Tiberius Kirk.

Captain Kirk and viewers alike were soon thrown into a space mystery. A species that can look like anyone impersonated one of the spaceship's crewmen, and, hungry for salt, sucked the life out of some of the crewmembers!

In order to protect his crew, Captain Kirk had to put the pieces together, solve the mystery, destroy the invader, and save the ship from doom—all before the episode ended.

The show was packed with action. Unfortunately, though, reviews of the first *Star Trek* episode weren't great. Some said that the sets, costumes, and even the acting seemed fake. But some viewers were drawn to the characters, especially Captain Kirk! He was tough and smart.

He wasn't afraid to show his emotions. He was in charge, but he knew when to ask for help. He was a space explorer who was still very human.

He and the rest of the *Star Trek* crew instantly connected with viewers at home.

Because of that connection, *Star Trek* would soon become one of the most popular science fiction television series of all time. And Captain Kirk would become one of the most famous characters of any television series.

But did you know Kirk wasn't even the show's first captain? And that the *Star Trek* series almost didn't happen?

This is the story of how Captain Kirk was created and touched the lives of millions of fans around the globe through television, movies, and more.

CHAPTER 1
Adventure in the Stars

During World War II, Gene Roddenberry was a bomber pilot who flew the B-17 Flying Fortress. After the war, he continued his career as a pilot. But on June 18, 1947, the engines of Pan American World Airways Flight 121 caught fire over Syria. The plane crash-landed, and the pilot died. Gene was the third pilot on that flight. He broke two ribs, but was still able to save a few passengers onboard before the whole plane burst into flames.

After that crash, Gene wondered if he should even be a pilot anymore. So in May 1948, at the age of twenty-six, he decided to pursue a new career: writing.

Gene had always dreamed of being a writer. He thought he could make money writing poetry. That was his dream—until his friend bought a new (and very expensive) piece of technology—a television set! In 1948, very few people could afford a television. Television stations were just getting up and running. There were only four hours of shows a night! But Gene saw something special on his friend's television, and it wasn't long before his dream changed again: He wanted to be a television writer.

He started writing scripts for different television shows, including police dramas like *Highway Patrol* and *Dragnet*, one of the most popular television shows of the 1950s. Many of

the television episodes he wrote were Westerns,
for shows like *Have Gun—Will Travel*. Westerns
told stories about the experiences of pioneers in
the Old West of the United States.

By the end of the 1950s, televisions were in almost every home—some of them now in color! Gene had become a well-respected, award-winning writer.

And now Gene had a new dream: He wanted to create his very own television show!

In 1963, he created a television series called *The Lieutenant.* The show followed the career of marine officer Second Lieutenant William Rice. Gene used his own military experience, through which he had achieved the rank of captain, to write a realistic show.

Unfortunately, *The Lieutenant* was canceled after a year. Gene had plenty of other ideas, though. In fact, he was working on something big! He planned to take what he had learned about writing adventure, justice, military, and drama stories and giving it all a science fiction twist.

Gene's new television series idea was simple but groundbreaking at the time—a ship would explore space in the twenty-third century. His show would be filled with a diverse crew on a space mission. He would call his series *Star Trek*.

Science Fiction

Science fiction stories take place in imagined realities. They can be set in a time or place in which science and technology are more advanced than they currently are. Stories often portray space

travel, time travel, or even life on other planets! Science fiction stories rely heavily on science and the imagining of what science could be!

Books and movies like *Frankenstein*, *Jurassic Park*, *Ender's Game*, and *The Hitchhiker's Guide to the Galaxy* are classified as science fiction. The *Star Wars* and *Doctor Who* series are two other examples of very popular science fiction. Science fiction stories answer questions like: "What would life be like if humans could easily travel to planets inhabited by different life forms?" and "How would culture on earth change with super-advanced technology? How would it remain the same?"

Having a diverse crew was very important to Gene. At the time, television shows only hired white actors for starring roles. He believed in a future in which all cultures worked together and wanted to show that possibility on TV screens across America.

But first, Gene needed to sell the show to the network executives—the people in charge of television stations. In his pitch, he described *Star Trek* using a popular TV show, *Wagon Train*, as an example: *Wagon Train to the Stars*. The crew of *Star Trek*, like the pioneers who first explored the American West, would make space discoveries while facing danger along the way.

Television network NBC was interested in Gene's *Star Trek* idea and asked for a television pilot. A television pilot is an episode that is created for the network to decide if they want to add a new series to their channel.

NBC logo

In 1965, Gene created the pilot and called it "The Cage." It told a space story starring the captain of the *U.S.S. Enterprise*, Christopher Pike. He was trapped by strange life forms known as the Talosians on their planet, Talos IV. The crew had to save their captain!

NBC liked the pilot. The science and technology were like nothing they had ever seen: transporters to beam people down to a planet's surface, force fields used to trap the captain, and aliens who could speak with their minds. But the network worried that the show didn't have enough action for the audience, so they rejected "The Cage" and asked Gene to give them *another* pilot, one with amazing science and technology, but even more action and interesting characters. They needed a show that would attract both viewers and the advertisers that helped pay for the show.

Gene had to figure out how to make *Star Trek* work.

CHAPTER 2
A Space Hero

Gene Roddenberry had spent countless hours and sleepless nights on the first pilot episode of *Star Trek* only to have it rejected by NBC. So when NBC asked for a second pilot, Gene began work immediately. He made sure to include all the ideas that were the most important to him.

He insisted that the ship's crew come from many parts of Earth and the Galaxy. And even though the studio wanted more action, the *Enterprise*'s main mission was still peaceful exploration. One of the biggest changes ended up being to the characters—their personalities and their relationships.

Part of the character change up involved recasting the lead of the show. After seeing his performance in the original pilot episode, the actor who played Captain Pike, Jeffrey Hunter, didn't want to continue with the show. He left the *Star Trek* project to focus on his film career instead. Captain Pike then became Captain Kirk, and Gene's next moves were to find a new actor for the new role and make the captain a standout lead whom viewers would root for.

The character of Kirk became an inspirational leader. He expected the best from everyone, especially himself. He was given enormous responsibility—to protect his crew and the planets they visited. Gene wrote the character to be young, full of energy, charming, and supersmart. He would save Earth from space dangers many times over. With Captain Kirk in charge of the *Enterprise*, anything was possible.

Gene felt confident about the future of *Star Trek* with this new character in mind. Now he just had to decide which actor could best fill the role. Many actors auditioned, but ultimately, William Shatner was cast and would become Captain Kirk.

After being cast, Shatner even made a few suggestions to Gene on how to make the character of Kirk even better. He thought Kirk should be a man with very human emotions. He thought Kirk should feel "awe and wonder" because of what he saw in space. Gene agreed to those suggestions and more and continued to work with Shatner on getting the character of Kirk just right.

In July of 1965, Gene felt he had everything he needed: a new script, a team of talented writers to help develop the show, a new lead actor, and a great story! Filming finally began again on the second version of the pilot, titled "Where No Man Has Gone Before." The story had more action, just as NBC had requested.

When the *U.S.S. Enterprise* attempted to break the Great Barrier at the edge of the Milky Way Galaxy, two crewmembers began to develop strange powers. The crew of the *Enterprise* had to defeat them before they took over the ship. The episode ended with Kirk reasoning with one crewmember and resorting to a fistfight with another!

William Shatner

William "Bill" Shatner was born on March 22, 1931, in Montreal, Canada. He is an actor, director, producer, writer, documentarian, and singer.

Shatner first started acting in plays at the Canadian National Repertory Theatre. He ultimately made his Broadway debut in 1956, and then acted in several plays, movies, and television shows before taking on the role of Captain Kirk in *Star Trek.*

Aside from Captain Kirk, Shatner is known on television for playing police officer T.J. Hooker in *T.J. Hooker* (1982–1986), hosting *Rescue 911* (1989–1996), and playing lawyer Denny Crane in *The Practice* (1997–2004) and *Boston Legal* (2004–2008). He has won two Emmy Awards—the highest honor in television—for acting.

Gene had given NBC executives, advertisers, and audiences exactly what they wanted. *Star Trek* was accepted by NBC. Thanks in large part to Captain Kirk, the *Enterprise* was now ready to voyage to television sets around the country.

CHAPTER 3
James Tiberius Kirk

Born on March 22, 2233, in Riverside, Iowa, James Tiberius Kirk grew up on a farm. He'd wake up at 4:00 a.m. to help his parents and older brother, Sam, with chores every day.

Nicknamed Jim, he didn't know much about life outside of small-town Iowa, but he *did* know about Starfleet. Jim's parents, George and Winona, had been officers in Starfleet, living a life among the stars. Both had served on the *U.S.S. Kelvin*, where his father had been first officer.

Jim and his brother, Sam, dreamed about a career in the stars, too. Sam wanted to be a research scientist, while Jim, like his parents, wondered if he could be an officer in Starfleet one day.

Starfleet

UNITED FEDERATION of PLANETS

The United Federation of Planets (UFP) was formed on Earth in 2161 by humans and three different species: Vulcans, Andorians, and Tellarites. Soon after its founding, the UFP created

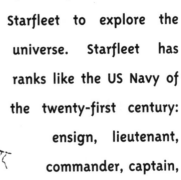

Andorian

Starfleet to explore the universe. Starfleet has ranks like the US Navy of the twenty-first century: ensign, lieutenant, commander, captain, and admiral. But Starfleet

Tellarite

isn't a military service. The crews on Starfleet ships are committed to gathering knowledge and connecting peacefully with other cultures. However, because the universe can be a dangerous place, Starfleet's starships are also equipped for battle. Its captains take an oath to "explore strange new worlds, to seek out new life and new civilizations, to boldly go where no one has gone before."

Vulcan

Finally, when Jim was thirteen, he had his first experience with space. He lived on a faraway colony of Tarsus IV.

When he arrived, he saw a peaceful colony he couldn't wait to explore. But out of nowhere, an alien fungus ate through most of the colony's food supplies. The leader of the planet killed thousands of colonists so that others could survive on the limited food supply. The planet was headed for destruction when Starfleet arrived with supplies. Jim knew for certain now that he wanted to be in Starfleet. He hoped to help planets—and find new ones—as a member of Starfleet.

When he was seventeen, Jim was accepted into Starfleet Academy's four-year training program. In the first eight weeks at Starfleet, cadets are pushed to their limits. They march in formation with heavy bags, run obstacle courses, take part in battle simulations, and are trained in survival skills.

Jim Kirk at Starfleet Academy

Jim's first year as a cadet was extra tough. Finnegan, one of the upperclassmen in charge of his squad, bullied him with mean practical jokes.

Finnegan from Starfleet Academy

It made it hard for Jim to focus on his training and classwork that demanded every bit of his attention. He was trained in everything from how to work in low-oxygen environments to hand-to-hand combat. He learned the histories and cultures of different planets. He studied the military strategies of famous captains.

Jim never gave up! By the end of his first year, he was assigned to the *U.S.S. Republic*. Jim was officially an officer of Starfleet: Ensign James T. Kirk.

He worked in engineering, the division on the *U.S.S. Republic* that made sure the ship ran properly. He learned quickly, and even found a mistake that could have harmed the ship.

U.S.S. Republic

Jim kept studying and training and eventually rose to the top of his class at Starfleet Academy. He became a skilled negotiator later in his career and was even awarded the Palm Leaf of Axanar Peace Mission for helping to bring peace to the planet of Axanar.

By the end of his time at Starfleet Academy, Jim was one of their brightest students. He became a student instructor and pushed the newest cadets to be their very best.

He especially made an impression on the Academy with his final training exercise. The exercise put cadets in the role of captain on the bridge of a make-believe starship to see how they would handle an imaginary crisis. Another ship—the *Kobayashi Maru*—was in danger, and the cadets needed to help! But, no matter

U.S.S. Kobayashi Maru

what each cadet did, the ship exploded, ending the training test. But Jim refused to fail. He hacked into the programming and changed the rules so he could save the ship! He had cheated the exercise, but still passed the test. The board of Starfleet officers who reviewed his actions commended him for his original thinking and let him graduate.

After graduating, Kirk was transferred to the *U.S.S. Farragut* as a lieutenant. He learned everything about the ship, excelled in every department, and was soon surveying new cultures on faraway planets. He felt confident he could do anything in Starfleet. But Kirk soon learned that there was danger as well as adventure in deep space.

On one mission, a strange cloud creature attacked the *Farragut*! Before Kirk could shoot it with the ship's phasers, the creature invaded the ship. Kirk was able to keep it out of parts of the

U.S.S. Farragut

ship, but couldn't stop it completely. The alien cloud drained half the crew of life, including the captain.

Kirk survived, but was weak and devastated. He felt it was his fault his crewmembers died. Kirk had never faced anything so hard, and he lost his confidence.

CHAPTER 4
Captain of the *Enterprise*

Though Lieutenant Kirk still felt guilty for the death of his crewmates, the new commander of the *U.S.S. Farragut* didn't think he was responsible. In fact, Kirk was commended for his bravery.

After recovering from the terrible attack and regaining his confidence, Kirk continued to advance in Starfleet. He soon became commander of his own destroyer-class starship, defending the Federation as he explored dangerous sections of the Galaxy. He also met and fell in love with research scientist Carol Marcus. The two had a child together named David, but Carol's and Jim's careers kept them from being together. Because Jim was rarely near his family as a Starfleet officer, Carol decided it would be best if she raised David alone.

Jim agreed, and he never saw Carol or David. He rarely saw his parents or brother, either. But all of his hard work in the stars paid off. Starfleet noticed Kirk's abilities and decided it was time to give him a new and exciting assignment. Starfleet Command made him captain of the *U.S.S. Enterprise.*

Captain Kirk became the youngest captain in the history of Starfleet. He was in command of the most respected starship, completing missions designed to expand Starfleet's knowledge of the universe. Kirk was confident—some would say *too* confident, but he would still worry over decisions that could affect his crew.

U.S.S. Enterprise

The *U.S.S. Enterprise* was one of the fastest and most technologically advanced starships when it launched in 2245. Part of Starfleet's *Constitution* class of starships, it is equipped for five-year missions into deep space, which it reaches traveling up to warp 8—hundreds of times faster than the speed of light!

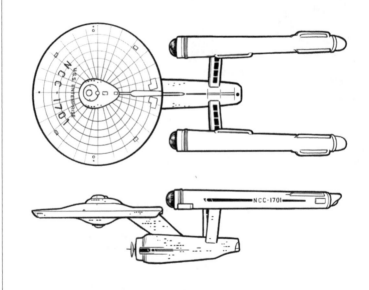

The *Enterprise* is an exploratory vessel; its mission is primarily to explore, research, and make first contact with new planets ready to join the United Federation of Planets. It is also equipped with phasers and photon torpedoes should it have to defend against any dangers. It has a crew of 203–430 depending on the mission. It is 948 feet long (just under three football fields) and has twenty-three decks, or levels.

The ship is controlled from the bridge, a large circular room on the top deck with different control panels monitored by various crewmembers. From the bridge, the captain gathers information from the science and communications sections and gives commands to the crewmembers manning the stations, such as engineering, weapons, and helm.

Captain Kirk was in charge of everything from science and security to engineering and navigation. He was smart, but he still knew when he needed to ask for help. He surrounded himself with officers on the bridge whom he could trust and rely on in times of need to keep his crewmembers and ship safe.

Kirk relied on his communications officer, Nyota Uhura, to pass his orders on to his crew and communicate with Starfleet, planets, and ships in many different languages.

Uhura had a wide range of skills that meant she could man the helm, navigation, and science stations in addition to communications. She once rewired the entire communications system to speak with Captain Kirk when he was stranded on an alien planet.

Hikaru Sulu, his helm officer, always made sure that the ship stayed steady on its trek through the stars. Sulu was a man of many talents who started in the astrosciences division. His talent for fencing was revealed when he was

crazed by a space virus and held the bridge crew hostage at sword-point. Kirk saw a leader in Sulu, and gave him a command position. He would go on to become captain of the *U.S.S. Excelsior*.

Pavel Chekov, Kirk's navigator, was Russian, young, energetic, and highly intelligent—in many ways like Kirk. But, like First Officer Spock, Chekov was scientific, extremely thorough, and highly logical. In fact, Chekov often took the science position when Spock was busy. He was an

integral part of any away mission, able to analyze data on his tricorder that allowed Kirk to solve mysteries on faraway planets.

Chief Engineer Montgomery "Scotty" Scott made the impossible possible. Known as a "miracle worker," he never let Captain Kirk down and pushed the *Enterprise* to new limits.

Like Kirk, Scotty was protective of his shipmates, but he cared even more for the ship. When a group of Klingons insulted Captain Kirk,

Scotty kept his cool. But when they called the *Enterprise* a "rust bucket," Scotty fought them!

Kirk's closest relationships were with Chief Medical Officer Dr. Leonard McCoy and First Officer (and Science Officer) Spock.

Kirk and McCoy were friends from previous Starfleet work, where Kirk gave McCoy the nickname "Bones"—short for "sawbones,"

Kirk working with Dr. Leonard McCoy

the name sometimes used for a doctor in the American West. When McCoy questioned Kirk on an order that didn't make sense or talked sense into him when he got frustrated and overwhelmed, the *Enterprise* was always the better for it. McCoy also kept an eye on his captain's health. Kirk would often push himself to his physical limits.

Spock was from one of the planets in the original UFP, Vulcan. Highly intelligent and peaceful, Vulcans are an honorable people who control their emotions in order to make logical decisions. In some ways, Spock and Kirk were exactly the same—both highly intelligent with minds that could solve problems quickly. But in other ways, Spock was the exact opposite of Kirk. Kirk was emotional and would often bend—or even break—rules in order to win any battle. Spock was unemotional and played by the rules.

Their two styles, when combined, created

one of the greatest partnerships in Starfleet history. Kirk and Spock worked together wordlessly—sometimes only a glance or a raised eyebrow was needed to exchange information.

Their relationship was more than professional. They were friends, though Spock would rarely admit it—to do so would be an illogical showing of emotion.

McCoy, Spock, Uhura, Sulu, Chekov, and Scotty always brought out the best in their captain and in each other. Kirk needed each of his officers to help make the *Enterprise* the best ship in the Galaxy and to help make him a legend in space exploration—one whose missions were now required reading at Starfleet Academy.

CHAPTER 5
The Original Series

When *Star Trek* premiered in 1966, viewers had never seen anything like it on television. The people who tuned in each week marveled at the technology in Gene Roddenberry's vision of the future. Space travel seemed possible!

On the show, ships so easily traveled to faraway planets, filled with new life forms and cultures. Fans gasped when they saw Kirk arrive on strange planets, appearing in the shimmering light of a transporter beam—able to return to the *Enterprise* with one call from his communicator. The technology seemed so real to fans.

While Captain Kirk commanded the *Enterprise* using futuristic technology, his training, and help from his crew, he also led fans through the plot of each episode. Audiences saw everything from Kirk's perspective. He began each show with an introduction: "Space, the final frontier . . ." and then brought audiences along on the mission through his captain's log entries. Viewers were eager to follow him to the next space adventure every week.

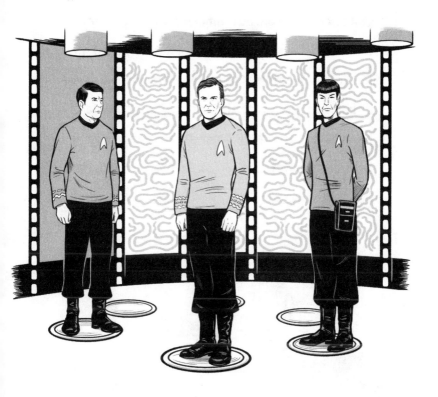

The Tech of *Star Trek*

The transporter was the most memorable technology introduced by *Star Trek*. It beamed crewmembers directly off the *Enterprise* and onto another planet. Warp drive and transporters are still science fiction, but some of the futuristic things created in the 1960s for the show actually exist now.

Communicators, the handheld devices Captain Kirk used to talk with the *Enterprise*, resemble cell phones. Kirk speaks to other ships through a screen with technology similar to Zoom and FaceTime.

The electronic tablets Kirk used to sign orders resembled iPads. Even some of the more advanced technologies, such as tractor beams (used to move other ships) and medical tricorders (used by Dr. McCoy to quickly diagnose patients) seem possible in the near future.

Captain Kirk was known to outwit his enemies during space battles—he once destroyed a giant machine capable of eating whole planets. He could solve mysteries and find alien spies, and could even survive on the surface of strange planets with nothing but his bare hands and survival skills. He battled the human-size lizard species, the Gorn, and won. He was a gladiator on a planet that resembled the ancient Roman empire.

He was even able to defeat an evil version of himself.

It seemed that Kirk could overcome anything.

However, during his adventures in space, he also saw tragedy. His brother, Sam, died when a space parasite attacked the planet where Sam was a research scientist. Kirk was nearly forced to kill his best friend, Spock, in an ancient Vulcan ritual, and had to fake his own death in order to save his friend—all while defying Starfleet orders.

His acts of leadership on every mission helped define the show. Captain Kirk was seen as the perfect mix of bravery and confidence. Wild, heartwarming, tragic, and fun science fiction plots from Gene and his writers were one of the reasons viewers were entranced by *Star Trek*. It truly was like nothing that had been on television before.

And even though *Star Trek* was set in the twenty-third century, it also addressed the scientific and social issues of the 1960s. One episode explored the issue of genetic engineering at a time when breakthroughs were being made in DNA research. Kirk went head-to-head with Khan Noonien Singh, a power-hungry warlord

and leader of a group of genetically engineered humans.

Star Trek also explored the issue of racism. One episode featured the first kiss between a Black actor and a white actor in a scripted television show in the United States—Lieutenant Uhura and Captain Kirk.

In another episode, half of the species on the planet of Cheron are black on their right side, and white on their left side. The other half of the planet's population have their colors swapped. Cheron had been at war for tens of thousands of years because one group thought the other inferior for having their colors swapped! The episode ended with the last two survivors of the war—one from each side—still fighting.

Star Trek was truly a unique show that captured fans' attention. They became deeply connected to Captain Kirk, his crew, and the peaceful vision of the future *Star Trek* showed. For some viewers, the show wasn't just something to enjoy watching—it was something that would become part of their lives.

CHAPTER 6
Star Trek Lives!

Star Trek was almost canceled after its second season, but the series had connected with fans who would prove loyal. Fans across the country sent in over one hundred thousand letters to NBC demanding the show continue. Fans protested in front of NBC offices in Los Angeles, San Francisco, and New York. In Los Angeles, a crowd of two hundred protesters held signs that said: "Save Star Trek"; "Star Trek Is Truth"; and "NBC Lives in the Past."

The fans eventually won a new season! NBC agreed to bring the show back for a third season in 1968. It unfortunately ended up being the last, with the final episode airing on June 3, 1969. Ratings were too low, despite continued fan interest.

But Captain Kirk, the man who didn't believe in losing, wasn't beat just yet. *Star Trek* fans weren't ready to let Captain Kirk and his crew go. Fans loved Captain Kirk because he was noble, stood for justice, and fought for what was right. They loved that he couldn't sleep, busy worrying about how his next big decision would affect his crew and ship.

So even though no new episodes were being created, *Star Trek* lived on after it was canceled. NBC offered the seventy-nine episodes to TV stations around the world that wanted to air it. This was known as "syndication." It made Captain Kirk recognizable around the world.

And the enthusiasm and admiration for Captain Kirk went beyond TV.

Books and comic books featuring Captain Kirk and the *Enterprise* were available since the show first aired. Captain Kirk was even featured in one of the world's first widely available video games. In 1971's *Star Trek,* a text-only game that people played on some of the first home computers, players took on the role of Captain Kirk and battled Klingons. The game, though basic, was so popular that by 1972 most computers had a copy.

Fans of *Star Trek* also bought collectibles, including Captain Kirk action figures, trading cards, lunch boxes, and T-shirts. Others even bought original scripts, film frames, and props used in the original series.

Most important to keeping Captain Kirk and *Star Trek* alive, fans who loved the show began to celebrate *Star Trek* at conventions around the country. People gathered to talk about the show. Some even dressed up as Captain Kirk or other characters! Smaller conventions, called "cons" for short, had taken place around the country as early as 1968. But the first major con—called "*Star Trek* Lives!"—was held at the Hilton Hotel in New York City in January 1972 with special guest Gene Roddenberry. The organizers expected five hundred fans—and three thousand showed up! The major cons became a yearly event.

There was hope for fans when *Star Trek* came back to television as an animated series also named *Star Trek* in 1973 and 1974. The original cast voiced their own cartoon characters. Animation, which allowed for limitless special effects, gave room for more unbelievable adventures. In this new series, Captain Kirk and Spock once again went where no one had gone before! They were transformed into water-breathers by undersea dwellers, the Aquans. The crew even beamed onto a ship with no air but remained safe using force fields. The show featured walking and talking plants, too! Fans were so happy to have more *Star Trek* adventures.

By 1974, the yearly *Star Trek* con was enjoyed by fifteen thousand people. Six thousand more waited to get in, but there was no room! Fans who wanted to *be* Captain Kirk finally got to *see* Captain Kirk. In 1975, William Shatner attended his first convention. Thousands of people packed the convention center to hear stories from the man who brought their favorite character to TV screens.

In 1976, *Star Trek* fandom even reached NASA. The space agency was introducing a new spaceship called the space shuttle *Constitution*. But *Star Trek* fans sent NASA hundreds of thousands of letters asking them to change the name of the new shuttle to the *Enterprise* after Captain Kirk's ship. They wanted to make sure *Star Trek*'s legacy lived on. NASA agreed! Fans knew how to make a lot of noise. But would their demand for new *Star Trek* adventures ever be heard?

Well, around this time, inspired by his fans, Gene Roddenberry started working on a script for a movie. Could Gene and his favorite Starfleet captain make it happen?

CHAPTER 7
From TV to the Movies

By 1977, *Star Trek* was more popular in syndication than it had been when it was first on air. More than one hundred stations around the United States aired episode after episode—some every night. But no new episodes had been made in eight years. Paramount, the company that owned *Star Trek*, thought it was time for something new. They asked Gene Roddenberry to create a second *Star Trek* television series, and he was soon hard at work on *Star Trek: Phase II*. He worked with set designers to construct a new and improved *Enterprise*; he wrote a new television pilot script; he reached out to the original cast to bring them back, and then began the search for younger actors to fill new roles he was developing.

Paramount had big plans for the show! They wanted to make it the lead of their new television network, Paramount Television Service. But launching a television network was difficult. There weren't as many channels on TV as there are today. In 1977, only three major networks existed: ABC, CBS, and NBC. Some Paramount executives soon realized that their new network wouldn't be able to compete. Plans for Paramount Television Service—and *Phase II*—were unfortunately canceled.

Gene Roddenberry had put a lot of work into *Phase II*. New story ideas and characters had been created. Sets had been built and new props and costumes had already been designed. Gene and Paramount realized that everything for *Phase II* could still be used . . . but this time, for a movie!

Captain Kirk and his crew were now traveling through space in movie theaters across the country when *Star Trek: The Motion Picture* premiered on December 7, 1979.

A few years had passed since Kirk led the *U.S.S. Enterprise* on its five-year mission. Kirk was now an admiral and chief of Starfleet Operations. But he still missed the days when he had his own starship.

The *Enterprise* had a new captain now—Will Decker. But when a mysterious energy cloud raced toward Earth on a path of destruction, Admiral Kirk took command of the newly overhauled *Enterprise* and headed into deep space to intercept the new threat called V'Ger.

Captain Will Decker

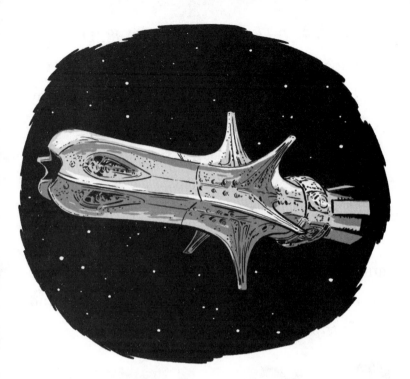

He gathered his old crew, adding in a few new members, and they all worked together to save Earth before it was too late.

The special effects in the film went beyond what had been done on the television show. *Star Trek* was even more exciting on the big screen! So, it was no surprise when five more movies were made.

Star Trek II: The Wrath of Khan (1982) brought epic space battles to movie theaters across the world when Admiral Kirk fought his old enemy Khan.

Twelve years had passed since Admiral Kirk saved the Earth from V'Ger.

He felt his days of adventure were over. He was now training cadets at Starfleet Academy. During an inspection of the cadets' first spaceflight on the *Enterprise*, an emergency led Kirk to command the *Enterprise* once again.

Admiral Kirk had to help his son, David, and David's mother, Carol, protect a new technology they had created—Genesis. This technology could bring life to lifeless planets! But the technology could also be used as a destructive weapon.

Khan had escaped the planet where Kirk had exiled him eighteen years before and was attempting to steal Genesis for his latest evil plan.

From Klingons to Khan: Kirk's Enemies

Kirk fought many battles in his Starfleet career, but certain enemies kept appearing again and again.

Khan Noonien Singh, in particular, was a common enemy of Captain Kirk. Khan was a genetically engineered human, known as an Augment. His intellect, strength, and endurance made him a perfect match for Kirk, who trapped him on Ceti Alpha V in the original series.

Cold and calculating, Romulans frequently popped up across the *Star Trek* universe, too. They are Vulcans who left their home planet, Vulcan, and its peaceful philosophy behind. Their "Bird-of-Prey" ships are not often seen by the

Federation. Romulans prefer to be out of sight while planning to take over the Galaxy.

But there is perhaps no deadlier enemy to Kirk and the entire Federation than the Klingons.

Kirk does not trust the Klingons, who seemingly celebrate war, chaos, and destruction. Kirk's realization that Klingons were planning an invasion of Federation territory led to Starfleet making him captain of the *Enterprise*.

Kirk rushed his crew of inexperienced cadets to assist, fought his way past Khan, and reached David and Carol. Things didn't go well for Kirk and his son at first—David didn't even recognize his own father. But Kirk did manage to defeat Khan *and* keep him from using Genesis, but only because Spock died in order to save Kirk, the *Enterprise,* and its crew.

It was *Star Trek*'s most stunning moment to date and Kirk's saddest. How would Kirk continue without his closest friend and most trusted first officer?

CHAPTER 8
Adventures in the Theater

The question of what Kirk would have to do without Spock luckily never had to be answered. In 1984's *Star Trek III: The Search for Spock*, Spock was reborn on the Genesis planet that had been created after Khan was defeated.

Kirk had to reconnect Spock's mind, which was stored in McCoy's brain, with Spock's new body. The first step was finding Spock on the Genesis planet. But Starfleet denied Admiral Kirk's request to use the *Enterprise* for the mission.

Kirk would stop at nothing to bring his friend back. With the help of McCoy, Scotty, Sulu, and Uhura, Kirk went against Starfleet orders, stole the *Enterprise*, and rushed to the Genesis planet.

The Genesis technology didn't work the way David and his mother had planned, and the planet was dying. Spock would die, too, unless they could get him off the planet's surface. Time was running out quickly!

But when they got to the planet's surface, Kirk had to battle Klingon commander Kruge, who wanted the technology for the Klingon empire. Thankfully, Kirk defeated Kruge, but the

Commander Kruge

Enterprise was destroyed and Kruge killed Kirk's son, David, in the battle. Kirk and his crew were able to return Spock to Vulcan, where his mind was restored, and Kirk got his friend back. But he had lost the chance to learn more about the son he had just reunited with.

Kirk couldn't grieve for long, though. He now had to return home to face his punishment for going against Starfleet orders in 1986's *Star Trek IV: The Voyage Home*. When he and his crew arrived, they found an alien probe searching for humpback whales on Earth. But there were no humpback whales left on the Earth in the twenty-third century, so Kirk and his crew traveled back in time to find them before the probe destroyed Earth!

The movie had a serious message—human destruction of the environment could have terrible effects for the future. And it was also considered the funniest *Star Trek* movie yet, with a very out-of-place and futuristic crew walking around San Francisco in the 1980s.

By the end of the film, Kirk convinced marine biologist Dr. Gillian Taylor to help track down and transport two whales to the twenty-third century. Kirk saved Earth once again. Still, Starfleet was upset that he stole and destroyed the *Enterprise*. Kirk's rank was reduced to captain, but he didn't mind. A captain's life is on the bridge of a starship exploring the universe—exactly what Kirk wanted to do.

Kirk was excited to sit in his captain's chair again, and audiences around the globe were just as excited to get back into theaters for the next movie.

Captain Kirk commanded a brand-new *Enterprise* in 1989's *Star Trek V: The Final Frontier*. Kirk, with the help of Scotty, was busy getting the new *Enterprise* ready when Starfleet called it into duty early. Kirk was tasked with investigating the kidnapping of Federation, Klingon, and Romulan ambassadors on *Nimbus III*. They were able to get to *Nimbus III*, but the ship was immediately taken over by Sybok—Spock's half-brother—

Commander Sybok

who had staged the kidnapping to steal the *Enterprise*!

Kirk couldn't stop Sybok from using the *Enterprise* for his personal mission: to find God at the center of the Galaxy. When the *Enterprise* arrived there, Sybok, Kirk, McCoy, and Spock beamed down to a mysterious planet and found an alien being who was pretending to be God. Sybok realized he had been wrong the whole time and put everyone in danger for nothing. He sacrificed himself so Kirk and his crew could escape.

Then, in 1991, the sixth and final *Star Trek* movie featuring the original cast was released in honor of *Star Trek*'s twenty-fifth anniversary. It was also the last *Star Trek* movie creator Gene Roddenberry saw, at a special screening. Gene died at the age of seventy before the movie made it to theaters.

Captain Kirk embarked on the final mission of his career in *Star Trek VI: The Undiscovered Country*—escorting Klingon chancellor Gorkon to peace talks with the Federation. Gorkon was assassinated, and Captain Kirk and Dr. McCoy were accused of being the assassins. Kirk had a history of distrusting the Klingons—even more so after one killed his son, but he would never ruin the Federation's best chance for peace.

Still, Klingon general Klang sentenced Kirk and McCoy to a prison camp on an icy moon. Kirk and McCoy were able to escape the prison, and Spock solved the mystery of who really killed Gorkon—General Chang and Federation traitors! Kirk beamed down to the peace talks just in time to save the Federation president from further attacks and helped create peace between the Federation and its greatest enemy.

Over the course of six movies, Kirk's adventures were bolder, his friendships with his crew grew deeper, and audiences around the world loved him even more.

Captain Kirk did return to theaters once more in *Star Trek Generations* (1994), the first movie to feature the new characters from the television show *Star Trek: The Next Generation.*

In that movie, Kirk joined forces with Captain Jean-Luc Picard to stop the madman Soran from destroying a solar system. Kirk battled Soran in a fistfight, and was able to keep Soran from launching a star-destroying rocket. But to the shock of many, Kirk died. He died a hero with Captain Picard by his side. Picard let Kirk know that he had made a difference. It was a perfect ending for such a brave character.

While Captain Kirk may have died on-screen, his character helped launch a generation of television shows, captains, and science fiction TV into new explorations.

CHAPTER 9
Captain Kirk Rebooted

After Captain Kirk's dramatic on-screen death, fans continued to enjoy the new stories of Kirk that were told in books, comic books, and video games. They continued to buy Kirk collector's items and get tickets to see William Shatner at conventions.

Luckily for fans, Kirk would once again return to movie theaters around the world. In 2007, it was announced that Hollywood producer and director J.J. Abrams had been asked to create a new series of *Star Trek* movies with all-new actors to play the roles of classic characters. In film and television, updating known characters or stories for a new audience is known as a "reboot."

Fans were excited to see Captain Kirk in the

reboot—but also worried. Many wondered how Kirk could be played by anyone but Shatner, who brought Captain Kirk to life over so many episodes and films. The actor Chris Pine had the same thought when he was chosen as the new Captain Kirk.

William Shatner made Captain Kirk famous and beloved, and Pine didn't want to insult him or the fans by trying to impersonate him. So Pine sent a letter to Shatner asking for his approval to play the part—and Shatner gave it.

Chris Pine with William Shatner

Worries aside, when the first preview for *Star Trek* (2009) was released, it became the most-played online trailer in history.

J.J. Abrams had a smart idea for how to bring the characters back to the screen without insulting or dismissing the original universe created by Gene Roddenberry. The movies were set in an alternate universe to the one seen in the original series of *Star Trek*. Each character still exists, but the new team of writers, actors, and directors were able to create their own twists to the *Star Trek* story. This meant that J.J. Abrams could pay homage to Gene and his space hero, Kirk, without making any changes that went against the original series, movies, or vision of *Star Trek*.

In the alternate universe, Captain Kirk's father, George, dies before he's even born. He sacrificed himself to save the crew of the *U.S.S. Kelvin* and his wife, who was pregnant with Jim at the time.

Chris Pine

Chris Pine was born on August 26, 1980, in Los Angeles, California. He is an award-winning theater, television, and film actor. Pine went to college at UC Berkeley, where he studied English and was in the theater department. Shortly after graduating, he began his work in television, on shows like *ER* and *CSI: Miami*. His first big movie role was in Disney's *Princess Diaries 2: Royal Engagement*, and he has since been in a number of science fiction and fantasy films, like *Star Trek*, *A Wrinkle in Time*, *Wonder Woman*, and *Spider-Man: Into the Spider-Verse*, as well as action films, such as *Jack Ryan: Shadow Recruit* and *Hell or High Water*.

Growing up without his father made Jim even more rebellious as a young adult. He joined Starfleet as a way to escape his life and honor his father.

In the new movie, the cadet Kirk finds himself on the *U.S.S. Enterprise* right after graduating from Starfleet. When the ship's captain, Christopher

Pike, is captured by Nero, an evil Romulan from the future, Kirk quickly finds himself commanding the *Enterprise* on a mission to save the Federation. He relies even more on his gut when making tough decisions. This new Kirk, like the original Kirk, makes bold choices and relies on Spock, McCoy, Uhura, Chekov, Scotty, and Sulu.

When the movie premiered, it was an instant hit and led to two additional movies.

Star Trek into Darkness (2013) saw Kirk grow as a leader as he takes on one of his worst foes, Khan Noonien Singh. Though he admits to Spock he has no idea what he's doing at times, he proves how far he'll go to save his crew and ship—he dies! (Though Dr. McCoy quickly brings him back to life.)

By the time *Star Trek Beyond* was released in 2016, Kirk is halfway through his five-year mission. He's even grown a bit bored and wonders if he should become vice admiral. That feeling quickly goes away after a new adventure in which Kirk and his crew save a massive Federation starbase from a new threat. Kirk knows his place is on a starship.

Overall, audiences loved the younger, rebellious Kirk and enjoyed watching the action-packed movies that added to the science fiction, wonder, and adventure that they loved from the original.

This new character was the same Kirk, but with differences that fans could enjoy. Seeing Kirk's growth in Starfleet was just as much fun the second time around. It was a wonderful way to bring a beloved character to a new generation—fifty years after he first appeared on television screens.

CHAPTER 10
Kirk's Legacy and Beyond

Millions of people around the world know Captain Kirk as one of the greatest space heroes. He's still considered to be one of the most decorated starship captains in the history of Starfleet and the *Star Trek* universe.

He acted as an inspiration and reference for starship captains who would come after him. After the original series, there were several new *Star Trek* series featuring several new starship captains: *The Next Generation* (Captain Jean-Luc Picard), *Deep Space Nine* (Captain Benjamin Sisko), *Voyager* (Captain Kathryn Janeway), *Enterprise* (Captain Jonathan Archer), and *Discovery* (Captains Gabriel Lorca, Christopher Pike, Saru, and Michael Burnham).

Acting as explorer, diplomat, time traveler, and hero, Captain Kirk is more than a recognizable character; he is a symbol of a peaceful future envisioned by the creator of *Star Trek*, Gene Roddenberry. Seventy-nine TV episodes, twenty-two animated adventures, and ten movies are only the beginning of his legacy. Inspiring engineers and scientists to create technological advancements; encouraging dreamers to dream of the impossible; promoting adventure and space travel; being brave, emotional, and smart; listening to the opinions of your shipmates;

and trying to make the best of the world, Kirk and his role in the *Star Trek* universe made him a hit with fans around the world that stands the test of time.

And the story of Captain Kirk is still being told. Plans are in the works for a fourth major motion picture in J.J. Abrams's reboot series. Books and comics are still being written starring this beloved character. TV shows in the *Star Trek* universe are still being made. There are always new items to collect—from stamps and limited edition coins to stranger items, like inflatable captain chairs for pools.

Fans still celebrate Kirk at conventions around the country. Perhaps the most unique celebration in the *Star Trek* universe is Captain Kirk's birthday party. Each year on March 22, a group of fans meet in Riverside, Iowa, future birthplace of Captain Kirk, to celebrate the character with food, Romulan ale, and games.

Kirk has become a permanent fixture in pop culture and science fiction. So the question is: What will the story of Captain Kirk be in 2233?

Bibliography

*Books for young readers

*Berrios, Frank. *I Am Captain Kirk.* New York: Golden Books, 2019.

*Cohen, Daniel. *Strange & Amazing Facts About Star Trek.*
New York: Pocket Books, 1986.

Goodman, David A. *The Autobiography of James T. Kirk:
The Story of Starfleet's Greatest Captain.* London:
Titan Books, 2015.

Ruditis, Paul. *The Star Trek Book: Strange New Worlds Boldly
Explained.* New York: DK Publishing, 2016.

Weber, Thomas E., and Emily Joshu, eds. *TIME: Star Trek: Inside
the Most Influential Science-Fiction Series Ever.* New York:
Meredith Corporation, 2019.

Whitfield, Stephen E., and Gene Roddenberry. *The Making of
Star Trek.* New York: Del Rey, 1986.